DIANA,
THE FAIRY TALE PRINCESS

Lucy Butler

For my family

CORGI BOOKS
TRANSWORLD PUBLISHERS LTD

Our fairy tale begins with the birth of a beautiful baby girl. She had fair hair and blue eyes. Her parents were delighted with their lovely daughter, and her two elder sisters, Jane and Sarah, were glad to have a new playmate.

The baby was christened Diana Frances, but only the fairies who danced happily around her cot knew then that her life was to be touched by magic.

Diana and her two sisters loved playing in the nursery. They had lots of toys, but most of all they enjoyed dressing up and games of make-believe.

They pretended to be three beautiful princesses, and they put on the prettiest dresses in the big clothes box. They never imagined that, one day, one of them would become a real princess.

Time passed by quickly and before long Diana went to school. She had many friends and, sometimes, like most little girls, she chattered to them a bit too much. Sometimes, when she was thinking, she nibbled her finger-nails, but she always tried to do her best. Her favourite lesson was History; she enjoyed learning about Kings and Queens.

The fairies smiled because they knew that, one day, Diana herself would be a part of the history books read by future generations of school-children.

Like all children, when she went to bed, she enjoyed a bedtime story. She often chose a fairy tale and she would snuggle down to read magical tales of a handsome prince searching for a beautiful bride.

When she fell asleep, the enchanted fairies kept watch over her. They whispered softly to each other because they knew that, one day, Diana's happiest dreams would come true.

Dancing played an important part in Diana's life. She practised regularly and did very well. As she grew, she became an excellent games player. She played in her school netball team, and really enjoyed swimming and diving.

The fairies enjoyed swimming too, but they were more used to flying than swimming so they all wore their arm-bands and water-wings!

School-days passed by quickly and it was time to move on. Diana had a special love for young children, so she soon decided to help teach at a nursery school.

She had become a very beautiful young woman and everyone who met her was captivated by her kind nature.

One winter's day, when the children arrived at school, they heard some very exciting news. The greatest prince, Charles, the Prince of Wales and heir to the throne, had fallen in love with Diana and had asked her to be his wife.

The wonderful news brought great joy throughout the whole country.

A summer wedding was planned and everyone prayed for a fine day. People came from far and wide and, even before dawn broke, the wedding route was crowded with happy people. Excited faces peered from every window.

Soon the wedding guests began making their way to the Cathedral. Kings, Queens, Princes and Princesses waved to the cheering onlookers from their gleaming carriages. Soldiers' uniforms dazzled and the horses' coats shone in the bright sunlight.

The cheers became even louder, the bridegroom, the happy Prince, was on his way. He looked very handsome in his naval uniform with his brother, Prince Andrew, beside him.

At last, the Glass Coach appeared, pulled by two magnificent bays. Everyone gasped and, for a brief moment, the crowd seemed to hold its breath. Then the cheers broke out even more loudly than before.

Diana looked so beautiful smiling through her bridal veil with her proud father at her side.

The coach arrived at the great Cathedral and, as the bride walked up towards the huge door, the best kept secret was at last revealed. The wedding dress was indeed fit for a fairy tale princess. It was made of the finest ivory silk with a tiny waist and full sleeves. It had a billowing skirt and a very long train.

For good luck, Diana followed the bridal tradition of *Something Old, Something New, Something Borrowed, Something Blue.* Old lace and new silk for the dress. Diamond earrings borrowed from her mother, and a tiny blue bow sewn into the dress waist band.

The trumpets sounded and the procession walked slowly down the aisle. To complete the marvellous spectacle, Diana had five beautiful bridesmaids with flowers in their hair, each carrying tiny baskets of flowers, and with them were two page boys wearing handsome Victorian naval uniforms.

Prince Charles smiled proudly as his bride knelt beside him. Even though the Prince was used to important occasions, nothing quite like this had happened to him before and he felt rather nervous. The bride and groom pledged their love for each other, and the Archbishop pronounced them man and wife. The crowd outside, listening on loud speakers, gave a mighty cheer. Inside, the Bridal Party moved into the vestry where the bride and groom signed their names in the register. Diana signing her maiden name for the last time.

The new Princess and her Prince now walked happily down the aisle together. The waiting thousands waved and cheered. The eyes of the whole world were focused on these two young people.

The long train rippled down the crimson-carpeted steps as they made their way down. Prince Charles helped his Princess into the waiting carriage and the bells began to peal. All over the country, church bells joined in joyful celebration. Grown men brushed away a tear, and strangers hugged each other as they glimpsed the Royal Couple. Everyone felt that they were guests at the most wonderful wedding of a lifetime.

After all the carriages had safely returned to the Palace, the huge crowds moved steadily towards the gates. Soon the whole area in front of the Palace was an ocean of excited faces, all waiting for the traditional balcony appearance.

When Prince Charles and Princess Diana stepped out on to the red and gold draped balcony, the waving flags and banners stretched into the distance as far as the eye could see.

The little group on the balcony waved to the crowd which exploded again with delight when the Prince kissed the Princess, putting the final seal on this fairy tale romance.

The good-natured crowds continued to call out for more balcony appearances, but inside the Palace there were still some formalities to complete.

Although the cameras had been clicking and flashing all through the day, no wedding is complete without the traditional family photographs. These were soon completed and everyone could relax at last. Far from the gaze of the adoring crowds, the champagne corks popped and the wedding cake was cut.

Then the guests and the rest of the Royal household moved into the courtyard to say farewell to the happy couple as they set out for their honeymoon train.

The Prince's two brothers had been secretly busy pinning a large *JUST MARRIED* notice to the back of the carriage and tying on a bunch of shiny heart-shaped balloons which floated jauntily in the air.

They were showered with rose petals and confetti.

Nowhere in the world was there a happier couple as they started the first journey of their new life together.

The Prince had found his Princess. A fairy tale had come true. That night, as the celebrations continued, the world seemed a friendlier place.

All because a young girl called Diana had captured not only the heart of a Prince called Charles, but the hearts of a whole nation.

The Prince and Princess lived happily together and our fairy tale ends as it began, with the birth of a beautiful baby. Within the year, a son was born to the happy couple, and like his mother he too had fair hair and blue eyes.

So just remember, dreams and fairy tales do sometimes come true.

DIANA, THE FAIRY TALE PRINCESS
A CORGI BOOK 0 552 99024 8

First published in Great Britain by Corgi Books

PRINTING HISTORY
Corgi edition published 1982

Corgi Books are published by
Transworld Publishers Ltd.,
Century House, 61–63 Uxbridge Road,
Ealing, London W5 5SA

Printed and Bound in Great Britain by
Purnell and Sons (Book Production) Ltd., Paulton, Bristol